Though I've traveled around the world, Toronto is the ~~~~~~~~~~~ 'll home. The largest city in Canada, it's ~~~~~~~~~~ residents who are hug~~~~~~~~~~~~ doubt notice bars and r~~~~~~~~~~~~ and beverage producers, ~~~~~~~~~~~~ homegr~~~~~~~~

An intensely multicultu~~~~~~ recognized and 140 lang~~~~~~~~~~~~~~~~~~here on the daily, and we Torontonians fervently display the influence those cultures have had on our urban home. From Chinatown and Koreatown to the historically Polish Roncesvalles and the Irish settlements of Corktown and Cabbagetown, no matter where you're from, visiting Toronto will likely feel like a home away from home.

Wherever you are in this city, you're in for an adventure. With this curated guide, I hope that you'll dig a little deeper and are able to see all the nooks, crannies and incredible charm that I've found each and every single day here in Toronto.

———

amanda scriver
writer

Amanda Scriver is a passionate freelance writer, community builder and body image advocate. Between eating and exploring everything the city has to offer, Amanda can be found writing words for publications such as *The National Post*, *THIS Magazine*, *Buzzfeed*, *BizBash Magazine* and *The Globe and Mail*. In her downtime, she loves a good cup of coffee, indulging in trashy reality television and communicating via GIF.

britney townsend
photographer

Britney Townsend is a photographer with an intense love for Toronto. Residing in Roncesvalles, she runs a local events publication, and is always seeking out the best new coffee, band and cocktail.

where to lay your weary head

Rest up, relax and recharge

HOTEL LE GERMAIN TORONTO

HOTEL LE GERMAIN TORONTO

Contemporary boutique hotel

30 Mercer Street (near Blue Jays Way; King West)
+1 416 345 9500 / germaintoronto.com

Double from CA$285

Want a friendly accommodation? Hotel Le Germain is for you. Priding itself on its Euro-hospitality, the lodging provides an incredible service from start to finish, helping your stay feel comfortable and relaxing. All of the rooms are spacious, modern and chic with deep soaking tubs, free Wi-Fi, Frette linens and Molton Brown toiletries. Do pop down to the in-house eatery Victor Restaurant + Bar – with a commitment to local ingredients and flavors, it's worth staying in for dinner at least one night.

THE DRAKE HOTEL

Live music and trendy digs

1150 Queen Street West (near Beaconsfield Avenue; West Queen West)
+1 416 531 5042 / thedrakehotel.ca
Double from CA$189

Since its inception in 2004, The Drake Hotel has been one of the premier places in the city to see and be seen. Located in West Queen West, this 19-room hotel is a go-to for globe-trotting tastemakers due to its eclectic and colorful design, happenings like curated art talks and half-price wine nights, and ability to keep things fun at the Underground, the on-site music venue. Watching the sunset with a cocktail at the rooftop bar, Sky Yard, is an absolute must. Also, the resident restaurant is one you for sure want to eat in. Chef Ted Corrado does an impeccable job at elevating comforting classics while keeping things approachable. Much like the hotel itself.

THE GLADSTONE HOTEL

Indie-designed lodging

1214 Queen Street West (at Gladstone Avenue; West Queen West)
+1 416 531 4635 / gladstonehotel.com
Double from CA$179

This revitalized Victorian-style building houses one of Toronto's most intriguing sleeping quarters. Each of the 37 rooms was uniquely designed by a local artist – there are such contrasts as 417, which is decked out with chinoiserie and subtle hues, and 403, a bright, Pop art-inspired space. Much like the décor, the amenities within each room differ, but all come with hypoallergenic bedding, premium cable, Wi-Fi and a Samsung Galaxy tablet to contact the concierge. One of my favorite aspects, though, is the charming, old-timey elevator, restored from the historical building's previous life, that takes you to each floor. The weekly events here are major and include contemporary art shows – there are three galleries – and trivia in the lounge. Don't forget to check out the Melody Bar or the cozy Café for brunch, dinner or drinks.

THE IVY AT VERITY

The sweetest dreams

111 Queen Street East (near Mutual Street; Corktown)
+1 416 368 6006 / theivyatverity.com
Double from CA$399

It's hard to believe, but these digs are so well hidden in the midst of the downtown chaos that I missed it the first time. But it's there, and it's a sophisticated oasis despite its location smack-dab in the thick of the city's hustle and bustle. Calling a converted 1850s chocolate factory home, this intimate hotel features only four luxurious, spacious rooms that are individually decorated, and each includes a balcony overlooking the dreamy, private courtyard. But that's not all: there are king-sized Hastens beds, Italian linens, heated floors, soaking tubs, organic bath salts and breakfast delivered to your room each morning. Rest and relaxation abounds.

THE IVY AT VERITY

THE TEMPLAR HOTEL

Upscale gem

348 Adelaide Street West (near Peter Street; Downtown Core)
+1 416 479 0847 / templarhotel.com
Double from CA$199

This 27-suite, eight-story hotel has seen many stars come through,
including Kobe Bryant and, unsurprisingly, our very own Drake.
But from the outside, you wouldn't even know it's a hotel – it's one
of this city's best-kept secrets. Inside, beautiful, high-end, teak wood
furnishings and floor-to-ceiling windows adorn the lobby lounge
and continue into the guest rooms, where you'll also find oversized
tubs, double showerheads and an organic mattress made up with
hypoallergenic, down-filled duvets and pillows. Hungry? Head down to
Parcae Restaurant, which lies behind an unmarked metal door at the back
of the hotel lobby and dishes up Mediterranean plates. Yes and yes.

THE TEMPLAR HOTEL

roncesvalles

bloor west village, parkdale, the junction

It's not uncommon to hear Torontonians proclaim that "the west end is the best end". Since I live in the west end, which encompasses Roncesvalles, Parkdale, The Junction and Bloor West Village, I'm fairly biased, but to be fair, this area has a lot of great history and has recently undergone much redevelopment, hence the excitement. Bloor West Village, a largely Ukrainian community, is west of High Park and very close to historically Polish Roncesvalles, where you'll still find authentic butchers and bakers mixed in with the burgeoning restaurant and nightlife scene. Just north is The Junction, home to many creative types thanks to cheap rent and the Ontario Railpath, an elevated train track that's been converted into a cycling and pedestrian trail that connects West Toronto to downtown. To the south of Roncesvalles is Parkdale – with a major population that hails from Tibet, North Africa and West India, this enclave is an up-and-coming hood, beloved for its vibrant, thriving culture and dining opportunities.

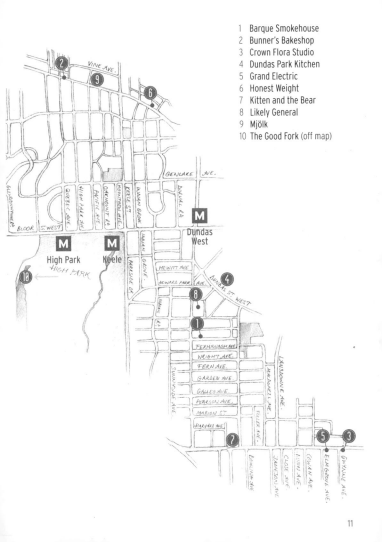

1 Barque Smokehouse
2 Bunner's Bakeshop
3 Crown Flora Studio
4 Dundas Park Kitchen
5 Grand Electric
6 Honest Weight
7 Kitten and the Bear
8 Likely General
9 Mjölk
10 The Good Fork (off map)

BARQUE SMOKEHOUSE

The Big Smoke's barbecue joint

299 Roncesvalles Avenue (at Geoffrey Street)   +1 416 532 7700
barque.ca   Open daily

You can smell it from down the street, and you can't help but inhale aggressively. Though Roncesvalles is popping up trendy restaurants like Whack-a-Mole on overdrive lately, Barque Smokehouse has staying power. On Sunday's Family Night in particular, the place feels like a Father's Day cookout. Episodes of *The Flintstones* are playing on the bar TV, each table has a bucket of popcorn for light, pre-dinner snacking, and platters of sausages, chicken and ribs are vanishing faster than Pop's hair. When you realize that the chef commutes from across the street, that friendly, family backyard feeling all makes perfect sense.

BUNNER S BAKESHOP

Delicious vegan treats

3054 Dundas Street West (at McMurray Avenue) / +1 647 352 2975
bunners.ca / Open daily

Even though I don't prescribe to a plant-based or gluten-free diet, I still find myself making the trek to Bunner's Bakeshop on a near-daily basis. The reason for this is that their confections are good (like really, really good), but it's also because I love their variety, from pizza pockets to brownies and, of course, cupcakes. While it's not the cheapest bakery on the block, you get exactly what you pay for: health-conscious, scrumptious baked goods. Visiting during the summer? It's worth popping by their Kensington Market location for the soft-serve ice cream, which you can get by itself in a cone or as an à la mode topper for your confection.

CROWN FLORA STUDIO

Blossoms and botanicals

1233 Queen Street West (near Gwynne Avenue) / +1 647 345 3567
crownflorastudio.com / Open daily

I was introduced to Davis and Adam of Crown Flora Studio was at an annual craft show. They were showcasing some of their gorgeous terrariums, including their amazing orb which comes with white gravel, reindeer moss and an air plant. I knew immediately that I needed one for my home and whipped out my wallet to make the purchase. If you have the opportunity to visit their shop and meet them, you'll be taken with how sweet, helpful and knowledgeable they are. With their keen sensibilities and floral design backgrounds, you'll be able to find the ultimate gift for just about anyone. My suggestion is, unsurprisingly, a dreamy terrarium – they have them pre-built as well as everything you'll need to DIY it, if you wish.

DUNDAS PARK KITCHEN

Homespun eats

2066 Dundas Street West (near Morrow Avenue) / +1 647 351 4793
dundasparkkitchen.ca / Closed Sunday and Monday

When Dundas Park Kitchen opened after a major renovation, I was impressed by the bright, beautiful, grab-and-go space decked out in a palette of light gray and white. I came into contact with owners Alex Tso and Melanie Harris when they were renovating – they kindly gifted my partner a fully functional, restaurant-grade espresso machine – and we eagerly watched their progress from the sidelines. Today, high-quality sandwiches and bakery items using locally sourced goods beckon. Behind the counter, the folks genuinely care about the food you're trying and are quick to make suggestions based on your dietary needs, likes or dislikes. My usual? One of their toothsome galettes.

GRAND ELECTRIC

Tacos and bourbon

1330 Queen Street West (at Elm Grove Avenue) / +1 416 627 3459
grandelectricbar.com / Open daily

Plenty of people (Torontonian and otherwise) have little patience for an eatery that requires waiting in line. It's understandable. If there were a reservation-accepting haven that served bourbonade and the finest baja fish tacos this side of North America, I'd put my name down for a table there far in advance. Since there isn't, I show up early at Grand Electric, Parkdale's most vibrant dining and drinking establishment (with due reason). When I do score a table, I have to remind myself to save room for the lovely little jar of tart key lime pie and prepare for the inevitable intervention that it will take to get me out of there afterward.

HONEST WEIGHT

By seafood lovers, for seafood lovers

2766 Dundas Street West (near Indian Grove) / +1 416 604 9992
honestweight.ca / Closed Monday

Can I be completely real for a moment? Honest Weight is the spot that my partner and I used to drop into when we were waiting for our laundry to finish its wash cycle. For context, owner John Bil is legendary in the Canadian food scene – in fact, he's touted as a seafood expert – and though the vibe here is comfortable and unfussy (the staff feel like pals), this isn't the kind of place you drop into while doing laundry. That is, unless you're us, apparently. My order is the okonomiyaki – a pan-fried seafood pancake stuffed with cabbage, Nagaimo yam and fresh fish, and topped with bonito flakes, cured fish and savory okonomi sauce – but if you're feeling extra fancy, order something custom from the fish counter.

KITTEN AND THE BEAR

Small-but-mighty jam atelier

1574 Queen Street West (near Sorauren Avenue) / +1 647 926 9711
kittenandthebear.com / Closed Monday

I've yet to meet anyone as passionate about their craft as Sophie Kaftal and Bobby Zielinski, owners of Kitten and the Bear, are about theirs. When I chatted with them, they told me all about their original range of jams, like the bourbon and vanilla bean, and afternoon tea. I had a feeling these two were on to something people would be obsessed with, and guess what? I was very right. Any time I crave the fluffiest scones, the yummiest spreads (the strawberry, raspberry and cream, and banana are all hard to resist) and a fantastic tea service, I visit Sophie and Bobby. A set for two includes a pot of tea, freshly baked scones, three original jams and clotted cream. If you don't have time to stay, you're in luck: takeout is available.

LIKELY GENERAL

Eclectic gifts from North American artists

389 Roncesvalles Avenue (near Marmaduke Street) / +1 647 351 4590
likelygeneral.tumblr.com / Open daily

Every single time I've walked into Likely General, I've been welcomed warmly by owner Brooke Manning's dog – I know this isn't true for all, but I am so totally into this because I love dogs – and that sets the tone for this divine purveyor of all things present-worthy. The shop, curated by Brooke, is set up gallery style, and the goods come from several local artisans. There's a little something for everyone here, as the venue sells everything from jewelry and cosmetics to housewares, bags and clothing. The store is calm and peaceful, and I legitimately want to be friends with the entire staff.

MJÖLK

Scandinavian & Japanese furniture

2959 Dundas Street West (near Pacific Avenue) / +1 416 551 9853
mjolk.ca / Open daily

It's not often that I leave a design store with a philosophical pang in my gut. But Mjölk seems to get me right there. With the most pine-worthy selection of interior items by designers from Scandinavia and Japan (plus a few from Canada for good measure), this store makes me want to cherish a cuppa in a Linum mug by Finnish designer Nathalie Lahdenmaki or linger over the morning paper snug in a Lamino chair from Sweden. With their impeccable taste and personal anecdotes, husband and wife owners John Baker and Juli Daoust make you feel like you've stepped foot into their private home when you enter this space. No shoe removal required.

THE GOOD FORK

Modern, seasonal nosh

2432 Bloor Street West (near Jane Street) / +1 647 352 5955
goodfork.ca / Open daily

Who can say no to comfort food? I know that I can't. One of the most reliable places for such fare in the city is The Good Fork. While the line is usually out the door here (who could resist red velvet pancakes?) for brunch, the dinner options are just as undeniable with lots of Middle Eastern flavors showcased, including a scrumptious hummus dish with smoked paprika. But if you're looking for something on the heavier side, try the stuffed mussels with farro and dates. They're aromatic, enticing and will not leave you disappointed.

espresso yourself

Make it a brewtiful morning

ARVO COFFEE
17 Gristmill Lane (near Parliament Street;
The Distillery District), +1 647 352 2786
facebook.com/Arvo-Coffee open daily

BOXCAR SOCIAL
1208 Yonge Street (near Birch Avenue; Summerhill)
+1 416 792 5873, boxcarsocial.ca, open daily

JIMMY'S COFFEE
191 Baldwin Street (near Augusta Avenue;
Kensington Market), +1 416 901 2289
jimmyscoffee.ca, open daily

NEO COFFEE BAR
161 Fredrick Street, #100 (near King Street East;
Corktown), +1 647 348 8811, neocoffeebar.com
open daily

ROOSTER COFFEE HOUSE
479 Broadview Avenue (near Riverdale Avenue;
Riverdale), +1 416 995 1530, roostercoffeehouse.com
open daily

SAM JAMES COFFEE BAR
150 King Street West (at University Avenue;
Downtown Core), +1 647 341 2572
samjamescoffeebar.com
closed Saturday and Sunday

Toronto's third wave coffee scene is not as large as some other cities , but the talent, passion and commitment the baristas, roasters and independent shop owners have is undeniable – they've wholly dedicated themselves to creating terrific coffee, from bean to cup.

That said, I have a confession: I only drink one coffee a day. Heresy, I know. I usually kick-start my morning with a macchiato or skim-milk latte, but I do love everything at **Rooster Coffee House**. The place will make you want to pen a novel or line a Scrabble board from one of the well-worn club chairs. The baristas are expert and outgoing, the regulars brimming from ear-to-ear, the vibe exactly the right blend of snug and comforting. No pretense, just the ideal wake-up call, whatever your brew.

You can't go for a java in Toronto without experiencing **Sam James Coffee Bar**. The venue (and Sam James himself) has a reputation, for being a bit crass, not taking itself too seriously and making seriously good cuppas by roasting beans from Cut Coffee.

ROOSTER COFFEE HOUSE

Boxcar Social is where consistency is key: on each visit, my barista has spent a considerable amount of time explaining every aspect of my beverage, from the flavor profile to the origin of the beans. These professionals are some of the best in the business, serving up a highly curated list of rotating roasts from suppliers across North America. If you're a coffee nerd, order a tasting flight so you can get the full caffeine experience.

Finding a good cup of joe in The Distillery District can be like finding a needle in a haystack. But look no further. **Arvo Coffee** has filled the void and provides both wonderful pick-me-ups and community. Owner Justin Carriere is trying different ways to change things up by creating original drinks; I love the sticky chai, with its hints of raw honey. If you have time to linger, tuck yourself into their "secret" reading nook and enjoy.

Smack-dab in the middle of Kensington Market is one of the most gorgeous, tree-filled patios around, and it belongs to **Jimmy's Coffee**. Here, the high-quality roasts from local Classic Gourmet Coffee and homey atmosphere are the major draws. The inside seating is intimate yet spacious, the type of place where you can as easily curl up and relax with a book as catch up with friends.

If you're into latte art, then you'll want to make a stop at veteran champion Bruce Ly's **Neo Coffee Bar**. He can be found behind the bar most days, pouring everything from hearts to swans into lattes. After you've gotten over the excitement and finally had a sip of the soul-warming brew, check out the pastry case. Co-owner Masashi Nakagome stocks the cases with an impressive assortment, but you have to try the Japanese roll cakes. Is there anything better than coffee and cake?

NEO COFFEE BAR

BOXCAR SOCIAL

bloordale village

little italy, little portugal, wallace emerson

———◆———

This budding pocket of the city contains some of the hippest places to see and be seen. In Bloordale Village, there's an entire annual street festival dedicated to showcasing all the tasty (and cheap!) eats and incredible boutiques this area has to offer. Then there's Wallace Emerson, a former industrial area that's been transformed into mixed-use developments containing everything from coffee shops to art galleries. Nearby, Little Portugal is home to Toronto's most visible ethnic enclaves; it's a place where you hear many different languages spoken while walking down the street and you're spoiled for choice when it comes to cuisine. This is perhaps why droves of young professionals are choosing to live here and are, in turn, bringing a new dining scene to match their expectations. As for Little Italy, there's the requisite pizza, pasta and gelato – meaning there's little to complain about.

1 Baddies
2 Easy Tiger Goods
3 Karelia Kitchen
4 Pho Lihn
5 Soundscapes
6 The Lockhart Cocktail Bar
7 The Monkey's Paw
8 The Steady
9 Woodlot

BADDIES

Aussie coffee and avo toast

679 Lansdowne Avenue (near Bloor Street West) / No phone
baddiestoronto.com / Closed Sunday

I used to run into owner Alex White constantly when he was a barista at Café St. Viateur. He always talked about opening his own shop, and I for one am thrilled he's finally done it — that is, established Toronto's first Australian-style café. The place doesn't take itself too seriously; on the menu, you'll find quips like "make sure you take a picture" and "our muffins are tops". Chef Alan Naiman has created a seasonal menu that everyone will enjoy, but my personal favorite is the smashed avocado with beet labneh, greens, sunflower seeds, pickled beet and roasted persimmons atop sourdough. Oh, don't forget to order a flat white — which is prepared by pouring velvety microfoam over a shot of espresso — to round out the experience.

EASY TIGER GOODS

Lifestyle and java shop

1447 Dundas Street West (near Gladstone Avenue) / +1 647 748 6161
easytigergoods.com / Open daily

This café-slash-clothing store is hard to go into. Not because it's difficult to find, but because it's one of those shops where you'll covet everything in sight. Curated by owner Zai Rajkotwala, this boutique carries a first-rate mix of apparel, jewelry and gifts for men and women. You'll find everything on the shelves from *Kinfolk* and Levi's to In God We Trust accessories and Province Apothecary skincare products, and you can even grab a mug of Reunion Island roast from the in-shop coffee counter to sip on while you're browsing. So get ready to bust out your credit card, because you're bound to find at least one fun thing you can't resist.

KARELIA KITCHEN

Scandinavian café

1194 Bloor Street West (near Pauline Avenue) / +1 647 748 1194
kareliakitchen.com / Closed Monday

I have wanted to travel to the Nordic countries for quite a while now. Unfortunately, the time has not yet come, but when the wanderlust is in overdrive and I'm craving a taste, I cheat and head to Karelia Kitchen: it's quaint, unassuming and, yes, serves more than smoked fish. They have pickled vegetables, fruit preserves, flatbreads and incredible sharing plates like their smokehouse platter – smoked Atlantic salmon, chicken, pork loin, rainbow trout and an assortment of the goodies listed above – which showcases all of what they're good at. Did I also mention they have a full fika (coffee and pastries) menu? Oh, yes!

PHO LIHN

Flavorful Vietnamese staples

1156 College Street (near Sheridan Avenue) / +1 416 516 3891
No website / Open daily

The pho wars in this town are in full swing. Controversy abounds about whose broth is the most satisfying and Ossington Avenue seems to be the epicenter of this heat, with two popular spots duking it out. Not that I'm one to shy away from a good fight, but my pick sits a tad northwest at Pho Lihn. Quietly producing some of the most moreish noodle soup around, it's the hint of cinnamon (I think. No secrets disclosed here.) and loads of fresh herbs that get me. This no-frills find has dark blinds in front, which make it look closed even when wide open, but don't be fooled. Come right in. There are eighty-plus warm-your-bones options to choose from.

SOUNDSCAPES

Music emporium

572 College Street (near Manning Avenue) / +1 416 537 1620
soundscapesmusic.com / Open daily

Wondering how a small shop selling CDs, vinyl and old DVDs can survive in our digital age? Drop in at Soundscapes for five minutes and you'll see musicians rubbing elbows with suits, and soccer moms buying tickets to the latest club show. This is not the kind of place where the staff will make you feel a tinge of embarrassment for never having heard Paul McCartney's first post-Beatles release. Soundscapes has unearthed so much musical gold, you can't possibly know it all. Forget Top 40 tracks – here, staff picks include Metric and Michael Kiwanuka. Not familiar? Have a listen via one of the three-disc music banks plotted all over the store. You can try it all at this candy shop for audiophiles. Wear comfy shoes; chances are you'll be staying a while.

THE LOCKHART COCKTAIL BAR

Accio booze

1479 Dundas Street West (near Dufferin Street) / +1 647 748 4434
thelockhart.ca / Closed Monday

Can I tell you a secret? I've only seen one *Harry Potter* movie. To say that most of the references in this pub devoted to all things Hogwarts are lost on me is an understatement, but hey — I love a good themed venue, so I stop by The Lockhart Cocktail Bar anyway. In the way of nibbles, there's the honey fried Horntail (spicy fried chicken drizzled with burnt honey and topped with pickled carrots) as well as the Forbidden Forest salad (artisanal greens, arugula, goat cheese, fresh veggies and basil vinaigrette). As for drinks, there are many "potions" and "elixirs" to choose from. I suggest the cleverly named Gin Weasley, a concoction made of Bombay Sapphire, Triple sec and orange bitters. Whatever you order, prepare to be spellbound and to have a fun time.

THE MONKEY S PAW

Unique bookshop

1267 Bloor Street West (near Saint Clarens Avenue) / +1 416 531 2123
monkeyspaw.com / Closed Monday

This is, hands down, the most fantastic bookstore in town. Specializing in 20th-century reads with a mix of all things paperback and hardcover, the shop places an emphasis on lesser-known works across different eras and genres. I can't count the amount of times I've brought dates here because it's such a good conversation starter. What I would recommend to anyone visiting is the Biblio-Mat, a book-dispensing vending machine. For CA$2 (US$1.50), you can take your chances and walk away with a delightful antique book – so I say, why not? With my money, I scored a title by the name of *The Dairyman's Daughter*, a 52-page religious booklet by Elizabeth Wallbridge that was popular in the early nineteenth century. The more you know.

THE STEADY

Vegan brunch by day, queer dance parties by night

1051 Bloor Street West (near Havelock Street) / +1 416 536 4162
thesteadycafe.com / Closed Monday and Tuesday

I love The Steady for a lot of reasons. For starters, it's a double-duty space
operating in the daytime as a café that serves up plates like eggs cornbrenedict
(poached eggs on orange jalapeño cornbread, bacon, garlic-sautéed greens
and chipotle hollandaise) and a breakfast tostada with scrambled eggs,
black beans, cheese, chipotles, avocado and pico de gallo. But all that changes
when it gets dark – the venue turns into an LGBTQIA-friendly hangout where
you can see anything from dance parties and comedy events to book launches
and drag performances. Touted as a judgement-free zone, The Steady is a place
I know I can head to alone, get some work done, eat a vegan doughnut and
perhaps make a new friend in the process. Not a bad space, if I say so myself.

WOODLOT

Wood-oven comfort food and bakery

293 Palmerston Avenue (near College Street) / +1 647 342 6307
woodlotrestaurant.com / Open daily

I'm by no means a packrat, but I have a hard time tossing outdated gadgets. If nothing else, they serve as reminder for how far we've come. When I go to Woodlot and look at their humble but gargantuan wood-burning oven on full display, I feel completely at home. Once you sink your teeth into ember grilled Hen-of-the-woods mushrooms or naturally raised flat iron steak, you'll question whether we've actually advanced at all; nothing beats cooking with old-fashioned fire. Though Woodlot is part bakery, part cutting-edge culinary experience, part neighborhood gem, it's, in fact, hard to define. But who needs labels when a place is this deliciously cozy? Forget sitting at home by a crackling fire — there's a communal table in sight of the main draw.

weekends are for waffles

Brunch for the discerning

There's no denying that Toronto loves brunch. At **Maha**'s, the space is homey, and the menu features several authentic Egyptian cuisine, including my choice, foole, made with mixed, mashed fava beans, diced tomatoes and onions, and topped with eggs, sunny side up. You'd be wise to pair it with black tea steeped with fresh mint.

Over the years, **The Federal** has become my go-to place for everyone's fave weekend meal. Beyond the comfy ambiance, the food is a truly great value for portion size. I consider myself to be a Cobb salad enthusiast, and this is the most superlative in the city. Not into brunch salad? Go for the French toast and foie gras – it's super tasty.

The White Brick Kitchen is my official "take Mom for Sunday brunch" venue. You'll find your typical eggs Benny or classic breakfast with two eggs, toast, potatoes and a choice of square bacon, sage sausage, salami or smoked ham. But I come here for their nods to Southern staples like The Big Jambon with buttermilk waffles, baked beans and ham.

Dining at **Colette Grand Café** is an experience: the entire restaurant feels as if you've stepped into a Parisian salon. The weekend brunch buffet includes everything your heart could desire: smoked salmon, tangy goat cheese, eggs, bacon and, *bien sûr*, sweet things, such as pain au chocolat, croissants, muffins and macarons. It's a French slice of heaven, but the kind where you'll need a reservation.

When my partner started working in the east end, dining at quaint **Lady Marmalade** became our weekly daytime date. For those with a sweet tooth, the daily baked bread pudding is unreal: think next-level French toast. For savory fans, you'll be into the build your own eggs Benedict. My choice? Spinach with brie, avocado and ham.

COLETTE GRAND CAFÉ
550 Wellington Street West (near Bathurst Street;
West King West), +1 647 348 7000
colettetoronto.com, weekend brunch

LADY MARMALADE
898 Queen Street East (near Logan Avenue;
Leslieville), +1 647 351 7645, ladymarmalade.ca
open daily

MAHA'S
226 Greenwood Avenue (at Sandford Avenue;
Leslieville), +1 416 462 2703, mahasbrunch.com
closed Wednesday

THE FEDERAL
1438 Dundas Street West (near Gladstone Avenue;
Little Portugal), +1 647 352 9120, thefed.ca
open daily

THE WHITE BRICK KITCHEN
641 Bloor Street West (at Euclid Avenue; Koreatown)
+1 647 347 9188, thewhitebrickkitchen.com
Sunday brunch

dundas west

west king west, west queen west

———◆———

The strip of Dundas West between Ossington and Lansdowne Avenues has become one of the most heralded and beloved neighborhoods in the entire city. While dining and drinking are definitely on the agenda when you're here, emerging artists have made their way into the area, transforming it into a robust and hip arts community – so much so that it's become the home to the new, eagerly anticipated Museum of Contemporary Canadian Art. West Queen West was bestowed the title of one of the coolest communities in the world by *Vogue*, and, well, I'd be lying if I said I didn't agree. With swanky cocktail bars, incredible restaurants and enthralling art galleries, this area oozes creativity and fun. West King West gets you closer to the glitzy entertainment district, and there's no lack of urban professionals taking up residence in the condos while partying on the weekends and buzzing around the active bar scene. In this cluster of creativity, you're bound to find a good time.

N E W S (compass)

BATHURST ST.

MARKHAM ST.

PALMERSTON AVE.

EUCLID AVE.

WELLINGTON ST. WEST

ST. WEST

WHITAKER AVE.

ADELAIDE ST.

NIAGARA ST.

KING ST WEST

QUEEN ST. WEST

ROBINSON ST.

RICHMOND ST. WEST

DUNDAS ST. WEST

BELLWOODS AVE.

GORE VALE AVE.

TRINITY BELLWOODS PARK

CRAWFORD ST.

SHAW ST.

GIVINS ST.

OSSINGTON AVE.

BROOKFIELD ST.

FENNINGS ST.

DOVERCOURT RD.

LISGAR ST.

ABELL ST.

BEACONSFIELD AVE.

SHRIDAN ST.

1 Beast
2 Bookhou
3 Drake General Store
4 Forno Cultura (off map)
5 Porchetta & Co.
6 Type Books

41

BEAST

Eat local

96 Tecumseth Street (at Whitaker Avenue) / **+1 647 352 6000**
thebeastrestaurant.com / Closed Monday

The name Beast might bring to mind a swarthy hideaway tucked in some back alley, not a converted house with a neighborly front patio and homespun vibe. Maybe it's that element of surprise that makes Beast such a delight. More likely, though, it's the care that Scott and Rachelle Vivian and their well-versed staff take to source local ingredients and conjure some of the most inventive dishes around. With plates like poutine with braised pork shoulder, strip loin with creamed kale and quail egg, and maple bacon doughnuts, Beast is a carnivore's dream. That said, vegetarians will be won over by their beet root salad and full Bodum French press delivered with coffee. Did I mention their brunch with a cult-like following? Hear me roar.

BOOKHOU

Handmade furniture and home accessories

798 Dundas Street West (at Palmerston Avenue) / +1 416 203 2549
bookhou.com / Closed Sunday and Monday

There's something about seeing beautiful, handcrafted goods that gives me a creative itch that I can't seem to shake; it makes me want to knit my own scarf or get messy with a pile of paint. Time spent at Bookhou brings this impulse out of me every time. This brick-and-mortar storefront for artisans John Booth and Arounna Khounnoraj feels like a real reflection of its owners. Everything here fits together seamlessly: the dim lighting, earthy hues, their studio space and attached family home. The wares, ranging from tea towels to throw pillows to wooden benches, chairs and stools are all made with such honest intent you'll want to support this pair any way you can.

DRAKE GENERAL STORE

Gifts they won't return

1151 Queen Street West (at Abell Street) / +1 647 346 0742
drakegeneralstore.ca / Open daily

Souvenirs the world over have a bad rap, conjuring images of cheap fridge magnets and shot glasses with airbrushed coconuts. Drake General Store has changed the game and reinvented the gift shop in order to accompany their cool-kids-only hotel (see pg 7) and restaurant. If you've ever wanted to bring back a present that doesn't scream airport desperation, here's your bounty. Nobody says no to a food truck cookbook or a cookie cutter that turns your toast wedges into actual soldiers. Finish up all your shopping with a portrait of the Queen smiling down upon you (yup, you're in Canada), then take a peek two doors down at Hot Hunt, a sister shop specializing in antiques.

FORNO CULTURA

Homespun Italian bakery

609 King Street West (near Portland Street)
+1 416 603 8305 / fornocultura.com / Closed Monday

Walking into Forno Cultura is like being instantly transported to Italy, even on the coldest, most blustery of Toronto days. Their secret? They pride themselves on using tried-and-true family recipes. The commitment to tradition definitely pays off because everything here is authentic and delectable – Nonna would be so proud! No matter the day or time, the space can be quite busy, but the staff are warm, knowledgeable and extraordinarily friendly. I usually grab a prosciutto and fior di latte sandwich, a mini-cake and a fresh cup of coffee to enjoy while watching the bakers work their magic. While it's not Italy, it will most certainly do.

PORCHETTA & CO.

Meat lover's dream

825 Dundas Street West (near Palmerston Avenue) / +1 647 352 6611
porchettaco.com / Closed Sunday and Monday

These days, young adults are often told to become multitalented in order to survive since it's rare that anyone works at the same company through to retirement anymore. Try telling all this to Nick and Vicky auf der Mauer, who own Porchetta & Co. and watch them prove you oh-so wrong. Their tiny restaurant is a one-trick pony of the most desirable variety: all they do is make really, really, really good porchetta. That's marinated pork shoulder, wrapped in prosciutto, wrapped in cured pork belly and slow roasted. You can order it on a sandwich, accompanied by a side or with a fried egg for breakfast. Toronto's carnivorous souls can be found crowded around the small counter in front, viciously guarding their rather messy spoils and savoring them before they have to head back to their multitalented lives in a serious food coma.

TYPE BOOKS

Well-curated page-turners

883 Queen Street West (at Gore Vale Avenue) / +1 416 366 8973
typebooks.ca / Open daily

Some people read books; others inhale them. There's a certain kinship among readers who value the feel, the smell and the experience of books, and in Toronto, this is where they congregate. I imagine that a modern-day Belle (of *Beauty and the Beast* fame, of course) would coast through Trinity Bellwoods Park on her bicycle, pick up a croissant and then spend the afternoon browsing the racks here, all before converting a beast into a handsome prince using some very well-written design tome. Type Books is the sort of place where the selection is so thoughtfully placed that you'll have an armful from the front table before you remember what you actually came in looking for. Bibliophiles, welcome home.

the culture trip

Art for all

#HASHTAG GALLERY
830 Dundas Street West (near Euclid Avenue;
Little Italy), +1 416 861 1866, hashtaggallery.com
closed Monday

ANALOGUE GALLERY
250 Emerson Avenue (at Dupont Street;
Wallace Emerson), +1 416 901 8001
analoguegallery.com
open Saturdays and by appointment

BLACK CAT ARTSPACE
2186 Dundas Street West (near Roncesvalles Avenue;
Roncesvalles), +1 416 388 7263, theblackcat.to
closed Monday

MILK GLASS
1247 Dundas Street West (at Skey Lane;
Lille Portugal), +1 416 536 6455, milkglassco.com
check website for schedule

ONLYONE GALLERY
5 Brock Avenue (near Abbs Street; Parkdale)
+1 416 809 6308, onlyonegallery.com, open daily

WALNUT STUDIOS
83 Walnut Avenue (near Wellington Street West;
West King West), +1 647 919 7336
walnutstudios.com, open daily

When I visited **Milk Glass**, I had no idea what I was in for – all I knew was that there'd be free beer. I've since learned that the artspace supports both emerging visual artists and fashion designers (Toronto's own Hayley Elsaesser has shown collections here), hosts book launches and has been known to hold weekend DJ nights. No matter your take on art, Milk Glass has it all.

Though the warehouse at **Walnut Studios** – a collective that's home to 45 artists in residence – isn't open to the public, they do have a program called Blank Canvases where the artists offer classes, including drawing, painting and creative making, which engages the community members in art and allows them to make their own wonderfully unique pieces. Check it out!

As it happens, a friend once lived with **#Hashtag Gallery**'s owner, Graeme Lucy. When he was brainstorming potential names and threw out "hashtag," I actually said it was terrible. Five years and one successful gallery later, #Hashtag highlights all sorts of talent, but it's the annual 4x4 show that I adore – every piece is 4"x 4"and priced under CA$40 (US$30). Last year, I bought a cross-stitched, fuzzy television screen, which hangs proudly in my living room.

When I lived in Parkdale, I'd walk by **Onlyone Gallery**'s colorful façade and wonder what was inside. One day I finally went in and found a contemporary art venue with exposed brick walls and high ceilings. Turns out, it's been home to some incredible openings, like *VICE*'s annual photography issue launch and an exhibit titled *The Rise of Marijuana* by local dispensary Tokyo Smoke.

As much as I love music, I never realized how much photography was a part of music until I walked into **Analogue Gallery**, which is filled to the brim with fascinating, unpublished images from rock history. Sometimes, the works on display are even taken by musicians themselves: former Broken Social Scene member Kevin Drew recently held a show of his photography works here.

Black Cat Artspace is always bumping, and, full disclosure, I held my art show, *Fat in Public*, here. But I'm not a fan because of my event – I love their commitment to social issues. For example, they put on a show about sexuality called *BikeRack*, as well as *Redemption Dogs* by Nicole Simone, which highlighted the relationship between owners and rescue dogs. Also great: exhibits are pay what you wish.

king west and queen west

In the very heart of downtown Toronto is entertainment district King West, which is primarily populated by high-end lifestyle shops, upmarket restaurants and performance venues aplenty. Folks flock here to take in a stage show at Princess of Wales Theatre, check out an indie film at TIFF Bell Lightbox or enjoy a night at the symphony. Nearby Queen West is, without a doubt, one of Toronto's liveliest hoods; it's chock-full of history and home to some of the city's most interesting and eclectic shops from cannabis culture to quirky fashion. Don't forget to check out the broadcast hub at 299 Queen Street West, where shows like news program *The Social* and afternoon lifestyle mainstay *The Marilyn Denis Show* film live every day. You can't miss it – there's a news truck that seemingly bursts out of the building's façade. If you look carefully, you'll notice the front tires of the truck spinning.

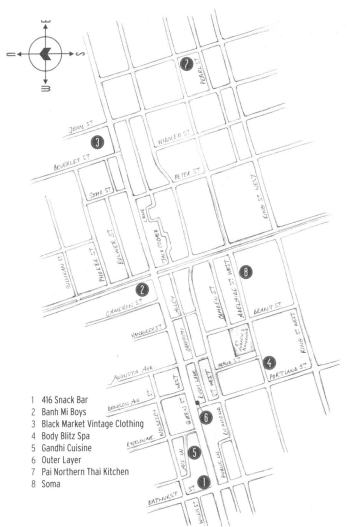

1   416 Snack Bar
2   Banh Mi Boys
3   Black Market Vintage Clothing
4   Body Blitz Spa
5   Gandhi Cuisine
6   Outer Layer
7   Pai Northern Thai Kitchen
8   Soma

416 SNACK BAR

Nosh from all corners of the city

181 Bathurst Street (near Queen Street West) / **+1 416 364 9320**
416snackbar.wordpress.com / Open daily

If you've had enough to drink, any greasy bar (or post-bar) food can taste like a culinary wonder. But how lovely to find an eatery where the fare is as remarkable eaten stone-cold sober. Adrian Ravinsky and Dave Stewart opened the doors to the delightfully divey 416 Snack Bar to fill Toronto's void of finger-licking late-night cuisine. This is no sad bowl of peanuts; instead, think tiny sushi pizzas or spanakopita. The zero-cutlery policy means all items are finger foods, and with most dishes coming in around CA$5 (US$4), you can get your greedy fingers on a bit of everything.

BANH MI BOYS

Vietnamese sarnies

392 Queen Street West (near Spadina Avenue) / +1 416 363 0588
banhmiboys.com / Open daily

Kimchi is an acquired taste for most Westerners. For me, the easiest entry point to the fermented cabbage is to combine it with the ultimate Canadian comfort food. Banh Mi Boys' kimchi fries are a strange but terrific Korean poutine. Lemongrass-braised tofu or pulled pork, kimchi, mayo and some other secret sauce on top of golden fried spuds? Gastronomical heaven. If you can't stomach the cabbage, their namesake bánh mì, steamed bao (dumplings) and tacos are all wise selections. Heads up, there will most likely be a line, but I promise the food is worth all your sighing and weight-shifting.

BLACK MARKET VINTAGE CLOTHING

So retro it hurts

256 Queen Street West (near Renfrew Place) / +1 416 599 5858
blackmarkettoronto.com / Open daily

As an angsty teen, Black Market Vintage Clothing was my go-to shop for finding unique threads. I would travel from my home in the suburbs and get lost in the 7,000-square-foot space that houes everything from kitschy Hawaiian shirts to nicely worn-in denim jackets and beat-up flannels. What's more, everything was (and still is!) CA$10 or less, so it totally fit into my angsty teen budget. One of my most prized purchases from here was a shirt declaring "punk's not dead". In this bargain basement of pre-loved goods, you're always bound to find at least one cool thing.

BODY BLITZ SPA

Therapeutic waters for ladies

471 Adelaide Street West (near Maud Street) / +1 416 364 0400
bodyblitzspa.com / Open daily

It's hard to put into words just how much I love women-only Body Blitz Spa. Featuring three pools — one with Dead Sea salt, a heated option with Epsom salt and another filled with cold water for an invigorating plunge — a eucalyptus steam room and infrared sauna, it's the ultimate self-care date, and it's hard not to get hooked on this little sanctuary in the middle of the city. To truly pamper yourself, book a full body scrub and have your skin buffed into super-smooth shape. After my initial visit, I couldn't stop raving about it to everyone I came in contact with for days. But if scrubs aren't your jam, massages are available with one of their registered massage therapists. The atmosphere is tranquil and luxe, and the staff are wonderful and attentive. Time spent here is pure and utter bliss.

GANDHI CUISINE

Delectable roti

554 Queen Street West (near Bathurst Street) / +1 416 504 8155
No website / Closed Saturday and Sunday

From the outside, this place looks small and unassuming – definitely not the type of venue that screams "Eat here!". That's why it's hard to believe that you can get the city's tastiest roti (Indian flatbread) here. But the fact is, you can, and they are incredible. I've trekked all the way across town simply because I have been hankering for their fare. The portion sizes are huge and the spices oh-so right. The roti wrap seals in all the sweet, thick and saucy flavors – you can't go wrong with the saag paneer (spinach with paneer cheese) or chicken korma. Ease into the spice levels though, friends.

OUTER LAYER

Things you didn't know you needed

557 Queen Street West (at Portland Street) / +1 416 869 9889
outerlayer.com / Open daily

Maslow was right about his hierarchy of needs: first you have to meet the basic ones, such as food (we have plenty of suggestions within these pages), sleep (check our hotel selections), and water. Once you have all that covered and you've worked your way up the pyramid, it's time to get the creativity and spontaneity going at Outer Layer. Did you know you needed a kickstand for your iPad? A brass knuckle meat tenderizer (how cathartic)? Perhaps a *Star Wars*-inspired cookbook? If you can walk out of this store without holding something up and shouting, "Did you see this?" to your shopping companion, I will buy you a watch made entirely of Legos.

PAI NORTHERN THAI KITCHEN

Authentic northern Thai cuisine

18 Duncan Street (near Adelaide Street West) / +1 416 901 4724
paitoronto.com / Open daily

In Toronto, Nuit and Jeff are Toronto's Thai food power couple. They met on the back of an elephant in Thailand and have since brought their love story here. Their passion has translated it into some of the finest, most authentic Thai nosh I've ever tasted. The menu is approachable, and the serving sizes big enough to share — an act that's highly encouraged here. That said, I love the gang kiew wan (green curry) served in a coconut and often do not want to share. Tucked away in the back of the restaurant is a small market serving grab-and-go meals not normally found on the menu, like guay jap (five-spice noodles with braised pork and egg), and house-made grocery goods including Nuit's Thai chili oil, which you can take home with you and use in everything you cook.

SOMA

Toronto's very own bean-to-bar masters

443 King Street West (near Spadina Avenue) / +1 416 599 7662
somachocolate.com / Open daily

I'm not a smoker. I'm a lightweight drinker. My vice? Crunchy, spiced pecans from SOMA. Once a bag is open, I'm a goner. Yes, I know SOMA makes chocolate – some of the most appetizing and artfully produced small batch bars and truffles around. Honestly, it's not just the pecans; I have a weakness for practically everything they produce. When a company dreams up such scrumptiously original flavors as Douglas Fir-infused chocolate and age balsamic vinegar and Madagascar cacao truffles, how could you not give them a whirl? (Did I mention Mayan hot chocolate?) Truth be told, I'm afraid to try all the yet-to-be-tasted goodies lining SOMA's decadently stocked shelves. Once I start, I know there will be no turning back.

for what ales you

Experience Toronto's thriving craft beer scene

Throughout the years, I've come to learn and appreciate the craft of a great brew. While I have gotten better at how to pinpoint my beer pick from a list of hundreds, I am still by no means a beer expert. Luckily, my hometown has seen the opening of several microbreweries that allow me to learn more ales, lagers and sours on the regular.

From the outside, **Bar Hop Brewco** doesn't look like it holds much promise. But looks can be very deceiving. This two-floor taproom has a lovely patio that looks out onto Peter Street, but that's not the reason you're here – you came for the 36 taps filled with craft hops on each floor and the fantastic array of bottles and casks. Their peach beer is summery perfection and the West Avenue Cider with cherries is incredible. Want to nosh? There are tons of snacks, sandwiches and sharing plates, including pig's head nachos. Yep, you read that right.

Bellwoods Brewery is Toronto's latest homegrown pub. Housed in an enviable converted garage with enough space for tanks, indoor seating, a killer patio filled with picnic benches and an upper-level deck, this place is not messing around. Owners Mike Clark and Luke Pestl got the vibe down pat. As for the beer, it's got the ideal mix of craft and creed: their award-winning Lost River Baltic Porter is heralded for a reason. This is the real deal. Bottoms up.

When I went to the beer festival Cask Days, I became a woman obsessed with cask-conditioned pints. Friends told me if I loved the event I needed to go check out their organizer's venue, Bar Volo. It was a beer lovers' delight. While they're currently moving to a bigger location, they're not neglecting their regulars: they opened **Birreria Volo**, a small, bare-bones offshoot featuring table service and a superb patio, and specializing in sours.

Everyone needs a local, and I feel very lucky that mine is **Indie Alehouse Brewing Company**. They're constantly changing up their taps, but the citrusy, hop-heavy Instigator IPA and the

BAR HOP BREWCO

BAR HOP BREWCO
137 Peter Street (at Jack Cooper Lane; Downtown Core), +1 647 348 1137, barhoptoronto.com, open daily

BELLWOODS BREWERY
124 Ossington Avenue (near Argyle Street; West Queen West), +1 416 535 4586 bellwoodsbrewery.com, open daily

BIRRERIA VOLO
612 College Street (near Clinton Street; Little Italy) no phone, birreriavolo.com, closed Monday

INDIE ALEOUSE BREWING COMPANY
2876 Dundas Street West (near Mavety Street; The Junction), +1 416 760 9691, indiealehouse.com open daily

LEFT FIELD BREWERY
36 Wagstaff Drive (near Greenwood Avenue; Leslieville), +1 647 346 5001, leftfieldbrewery.ca open daily

Order up a beer flight: you can choose five different styles to try. Whatever you go with, you're in for a good time.

Mark and Mandie Murphy love two things: baseball and craft beer. It's no wonder, then, that they got into the brewing business and named their venture after their favorite sport. Tucked away in an alley, **Left Field Brewery** this is a place for excellent pints. Try the Eephus, a dark, creamy oatmeal ale named after a rare pitching style, or the Wrigley, an oat pale ale with hints of orange, pine and honey, named after the owner's dog (and the famous Chicago baseball stadium).

chinatown

kensington market

One of Toronto's most vibrant and singular neighborhoods, Kensington Market is nestled within Chinatown. In the 1920s, the Market (as it's known by locals) was called Jewish Market since many of the bakery owners and tailors were, no surprise here, Jewish. Today, a visit to the Market's purveyors is like taking a sensory trip way south: many Portuguese and Latin American store owners call it home. I love coming by on the semiannual Pedestrian Sundays, when the roads are closed and the true eclecticism of this area spills out into the streets. A few blocks over is one of the largest Chinatowns in North America. Walking through, you'll find the streets buzzing with vendors hawking exotic fruits and makers selling cultural handicrafts. With a wide variety of Asian cultures represented, the visit is always one that's rewarding and delicious.

1 1/2 oz. Cocktail Emporium
2 Courage My Love
3 Good Egg
4 King's Noodle Restaurant
5 Mother's Dumplings
6 Otto's Berlin Döner
7 Seven Lives Tacos Y Mariscos
8 Urban Herbivore

1/2 OZ. COCKTAIL EMPORIUM

Shake it up

20 Kensington Avenue (at Fitzroy Terrace) / +1 647 729 9986
cocktailemporium.ca / Open daily

You won't be able to miss this purveyor: it's bright pink, and I cannot find enough words to adequately express how much I adore it. For those who love to imbibe, this store is like Santa's workshop. There's a little something for every home mixologist, no matter your beverage proclivities. From bitters, syrups, ingredient kits, DIY accessories and even glassware from yesteryear, this stockist of hooch accessories has a marvelous array of items no matter where you are in your cocktail journey. Their tiki mug in the shape of a panda is one of my most treasured items. Nothing makes booze taste better than cute barware.

COURAGE MY LOVE

Throwback trinkets and threads

14 Kensington Avenue (near Dundas Street West) / +1 416 979 1992
facebook.com/pages/Courage-My-Love / Open daily

While there are many secondhand stores to choose from in the Market, Courage My Love somehow does it better than most. I can kill hours in the enormous store, rummaging through their well-curated sartorial selection and admiring the options from jackets to dresses. But this place packs in more than clothes; there are also piles of groovy tchotchkes waiting for the opportunity to provide that extra whimsical kick to your place, and loads of costume jewelry to take your next formal event (or themed party) to the next level. My suggestion, though: check out the shoe racks. Last time I went, I snapped up a pair of Doc Martens in good condition for super cheap. Major score.

GOOD EGG

Fab kitchenware

267 Augusta Avenue (near Nassau Street) / +1 416 593 4663
goodegg.ca / Open daily

There are a gazillion cookbooks out there. At least, it certainly feels like
that sometimes. I, for one, can't get enough. Especially when the store has
a well-honed selection, and particularly if that store is Good Egg. Deemed
a shop for people who like to eat, this venue is all that and way more: an
outlet to stock up on Marimekko tea towels or that beautifully oiled butcher
block from Cape Breton you've had your eye on, Good Egg will make you
strive to be the next culinary superstar – or at least someone who can whip
together a pretty decent meal. Whatever you fancy, this place will have you
feeling well-read and well-fed from every angle. Bon appétit!

KING'S NOODLE RESTAURANT

Believe the hype

296 Spadina Avenue (near Dundas Street West) / +1 416 598 1817
kingsnoodle.ca / Closed Wednesday

This noodle slinger was packed out long before American television personality Andrew Zimmern gave it a cosign. His endorsement wasn't telling locals anything we didn't already know, which is that this is the place to go if you want a true Chinatown experience in Toronto – it just means that it's busier. But, it's so good you won't even mind the crowd. You'll see fresh, glistening, barbecued ducks hanging in the windows, and though the menu is massive, don't feel overwhelmed; much of it features different takes on the gargantuan portions of exceptional pork and fowl. My pick is their barbecued duck and three-style barbecue pork, but, to be fair, you could order anything from here and be happy and satisfied.

MOTHER'S DUMPLINGS

Chinese bao house

421 Spadina Avenue (near College Street) | +1 416 217 2008
mothersdumplings.com | Open daily

Toronto's restaurant scene has become a little crazy. Sure, it's awesome to
be the first of your friends to try the hottest new place, but what about
the nights when you need to squeeze a birthday party of 12 into one
table without bowing down to the sad neon lights of a mid-level chain?
When the going gets tough, the tough get dumplings. Mother's Dumplings
puts all the loving care you'd expect from such a name into their tender
little pockets of flavor, sans pretension. The menu includes pan-fried,
boiled and steamed varieties, but if I had to choose favorites, it'd be the
steamed pork and chive and the steamed melon, tofu and vegetable noodle.
If you're seated toward the back, you can even see the creation in action
through a small glass partition – though the speed of these masters' hands
is akin to a hummingbird's wings. Pass the soy sauce, please.

OTTO'S BERLIN DÖNER

Berlin-style street food

256 Augusta Avenue (near Oxford Street) / +1 647 347 7713
ottosdoner.com / Open daily

I know this joint's owners, Nancy and Konrad, from back when they used to throw raves in tiny dim sum restaurants. The concept lead them to eventually open their own eatery and, well, it has a weird, rave-like component to it (let's just say you'll smile – and laugh – when you go to the restroom). Canadians tend to be very territorial over our Halifax donair, which is served in a pita with spiced, roasted ground beef and topped with tomatoes, raw onions and a bewitching evaporated milk-vinegar-garlic sauce. So when Otto's Berlin Döner launched, I was stoked to compare this sucker to the Halifax version. Though similar in theory, the two are wholly different. My verdict? The Berlin import is really freaking good. This veal and lamb döner is served open-face on an herbaceous bread and topped with sliced, spit-roasted meat and an abundance of lettuce, tomato, onions and a yogurt-based garlic sauce. Psst: there's also currywurst here.

SEVEN LIVES TACOS Y MARISCOS

Viva comida

69 Kensington Avenue (near St Andrew Street) / +1 416 803 1085
facebook.com/SevenLivesTacosYMariscos / Open daily

Back in the day, monthly food event Toronto Underground Market was where many aspiring restaurateurs would introduce their recipes, dishing out from stalls. I got hooked on the goods from this taqueria there and I've been scarfing their Tijuana-style tacos ever since. Though Mexican eateries are a dime a dozen, Seven Lives differs from the rest. The tacos at this cash-only joint are made with fresh ingredients, including house-made tortillas. Take, for example, my personal pick – the Gobernador – made with house-smoked tuna, grilled shrimp and creamy cheese. *Tu quieres* Seven Lives Tacos Y Mariscos now, right?

URBAN HERBIVORE

All things veggie

64 Oxford Street (at Augusta Avenue) / +1 416 927 1231
herbivore.to / Open daily

A few years ago, people lost their free-trade, organic minds when an ubiquitous coffee shop opened a location in the Market. It's the one place in the city where the reaction was justified – compared to local institutions, the chain was akin to a swarm of locusts closing in on that last little green patch. This area was gluten-free and vegan before it was cool, and even my meat-loving friends will concede that the sandwiches at Urban Herbivore aren't missing a thing. Piled with fresh veggies on olive focaccia or rosemary bread (baked in-house), there are no post-lunch hunger pangs in sight after you've snarfed the barbecue tofu with marinated tomatoes, pickled cucumbers, sprouts, red leaf lettuce and tahini. So the big chains can continue to eat their hearts out...Urban Herbivore wouldn't cook with those kinds of ingredients anyway.

bites on a budget

Wallet-friendly nosh

BOBBIE SUE'S MAC + CHEESE
162 Ossington Avenue (at Foxley Street;
West Queen West), +1 647 352 2762, bobbiesues.com
open daily

NAZARETH ETHIOPIAN RESTAURANT
969 Bloor Street West (near Dovercourt Road;
Wallace Emerson), +1 416 535 0797
facebook.com/pages/Nazareth-Restaurant
closed Tuesday

POUTINI'S HOUSE OF POUTINE
1112 Queen Street West (near Lisgar Street;
West Queen West), +1 647 342 3732, poutini.com
open daily

RASTA PASTA
61 Kensington Avenue (near St Andrew Street;
Kensington Market), +1 647 501 4505
eatrastapasta.ca, closed Monday

WHEN THE PIG CAME HOME
3035 Dundas Street West (at High Park Avenue;
The Junction), +1 647 345 9001
facebook.com/people/Pig-Came-Home
closed Monday

If you were like me, you were raised with dinners that often came from a branded box. (Ain't no shame in that.) Though I eat healthier than that now, I sometimes find myself having one-off cravings for food that isn't so good for me. Luckily, Toronto can deliver.

Brothers Nicholas and Frederic Laliberté seem to have comfort food down to a science with their two eateries dedicated to North American classics. **Bobbie Sue's Mac + Cheese** has the five-cheese blend you're after, but it's the creative combos like carbonara mac (pancetta, grana padano and egg yolk) or Hamburger Who Lends a Hand Mac (hamburger, Gruyère and mushrooms) that keep me coming back. Well that, and the fact that you can eat here for under CA$15 (US$12).

Their second venture is all about poutine – fries topped with deep-fried "squeaky" cheese curds and gravy. For a well-crafted, handmade version, **Poutini's House of Poutine** is the place: the fare is always on point and worth every artery-clogging bite. I recommend the roasted mushroom + onion (CA$9; US$7) or The Works, topped with sour cream, bacon and chives (CA$11; US$8).

A friend introduced me to flavorful wonder **Nazareth Ethiopian Restaurant**. I usually opt for the huge vegetarian platter (slow-cooked lentils, split peas and atkilt wot, made with spiced cabbage, carrot and potato) all beautifully seasoned and served with injera, an East African flatbread. Split it with a friend for a scrumptious dinner under CA$20 (US$15).

Rasta Pasta's Italian-Caribbean fusion might sound strange, but once you inhale the aroma wafting out of the windows, you'll get it. When you score your box of takeout, you'll be pleased to discover that the meat literally falls off the bone and the taste is superb. The small jerk chicken is a steal at CA$6 (US$4.50), but for the true experience, try their Irie fettuccine – jerk chicken, fettuccine and alfredo sauce. It's a game changer.

As it happens, Josh from Schmaltz Appetizing (see pg 80) recommended **When the Pig Came Home** to me. Their small menu packs a punch, and the crowning jewel of a sandwich is the Toronto peameal bacon, which is cured in-house, served on a bun with maple aioli, tomato and kale, and will only set you back CA$5 (US$4). My recommendation though? The Montreal-style smoked meat (CA$9; US$7), which gives Schwartz's in Montreal a run for its money.

koreatown

the annex, yorkville

Stretching between West Bloor West and Dupont Street, the area around the University of Toronto is known as The Annex. This economical area sports many sushi joints and cafés that cater to the college crowd. If that's not your scene, stroll down to Koreatown, just west of The Annex. Home to some 50,000 Korean-Canadians, it's no surprise that many businesses here accommodate the needs of the Korean community, but there are also board game cafés, bakeries, indoor rock climbing and yes, you guessed it – karaoke. On the eastern side of The Annex is Yorkville, which was the original home of the buzzy Toronto International Film Festival. It used to be common to see the likes of Eddie Murphy, Rod Stewart and Renée Zellweger hanging in bars and restaurants here. Nowadays, the vibe of to-see-and-be-seen still pervades, but designer boutiques and dining establishments are the true stars here.

1 Bar Reyna
2 Basecamp Climbing
3 Schmaltz Appetizing
4 Snakes & Lattes
5 Tacos El Asador
6 XO Karaoke

BAR REYNA

All hail this cocktail bar

**158 Cumberland Street (near Old York Lane) / +1 647 748 4464
barreyna.com / Open daily**

Restaurant-industry veteran Nicki Laborie is the type of person who never forgets a face. She's a queen at recognizing folks and being the life of the party. So it seemed natural when Nicki opened up Bar Reyna. If you're looking to tour the Mediterranean, there is no need to get your passport stamped because all the bases are covered here. I love to imbibe Her Royal Highness (vodka, Mount Gay XO, saffron, cardamom, rose water, orgeat, grapefruit and a citrus blend), which is served in a large copper pineapple, and savor the star dish, The Cataplana. It's loaded with lobster, shrimp, clams, mussels and monkfish. Ready to pledge your fealty yet?

BASECAMP CLIMBING

Belay on

677 Bloor Street West (near Manning Avenue) / +1 416 855 0430
basecampclimbing.ca / Open daily

Fun fact: this rock climbing gym was once home to a seedy porn theater. After undergoing a complete (and very thorough) renovation, you'll now find the tallest climbing walls in Toronto here. The experienced usually jump right in – or up, as it were – but if you're like me and have little-to-no experience, don't be afraid. The staff here are incredible at getting you started and making sure your time on the wall is top notch. The 7,000-square-foot gym has tons of space and challenge levels, allowing you to mix up the types of walls you tackle. So strap on your harness and helmet, and get your climb on.

SCHMALTZ APPETIZING

Russ & Daughters who?

414 Dupont Street (near Howland Avenue) / +1 647 350 4261
schmaltzappetizing.com / Open daily

Each and every time you come to Schmaltz Appetizing, you'll run into manager Josh Charbonneau (and maybe celebrity chef-owner Anthony Rose) behind the counter. Josh will greet you with one of the warmest welcomes ever, at a restaurant or otherwise. Besides the grab-and-go bagels, Josh is one of the reasons I come here. He'll walk you through (and let you taste) everything behind the counter that day, which usually consists of delicacies like chopped liver, smoked fishes, labneh and hummus, but the real stars are the bagels. The massive suckers come with a multitude of topper options, but one reigns supreme: the smoked pastrami salmon. It truly is bagel porn.

SNAKES & LATTES

Late-night board games

600 Bloor Street West (near Palmerston Avenue) / +1 647 342 9229
snakesandlattes.com / Open daily

Sometimes, the usual after-dark activities of our times aren't so appealing. I definitely have nights where I don't want to dance around a pile of purses to deafening club beats, or sit at a bar being hit on. Snakes & Lattes is the mecca of alternative social gatherings; a café where you can play any of a selection of hundreds of board games for a minimal entry fee. For all you lot who have been secretly playing Settlers of Catan, your time to be cool has come. For the rest of us, get here early and settle in with a little game called Cards Against Humanity. I dare you not to spend the night laughing until you cry.

TACOS EL ASADOR

Authentic Salvadoran cuisine

690 Bloor Street West (at Clinton Street) / +1 416 538 9747
facebook.com/Tacos-El-Asador / Closed Wednesday

This is undoubtedly one of my fave spots in Toronto for tacos. When I was a very broke student, Tacos El Asador was my go-to. Though there's not a single frill, the setup with picnic tables for communal eating feels cute and cozy. If you're coming in here looking for real authentic Mexican, you'll be disappointed, but what they do serve is Salvadoran fare, and they do it well. The pupusas and tamales are so toothsome, you'll seek me out to thank me later. Tacos are under CA$4 (US$3) apiece, and you'll find al pastor (pork), chorizo, fish and chicken available. An entire meal for well under CA$15 (US$12) – not bad, right?

XO KARAOKE

Channel your inner Beyoncé

693 Bloor Street West (at Clinton Street) / +1 416 535 3734
facebook.com/XO-Karaoke / Open daily

If you're looking for a fun, weird night out where you can sing a few
Spice Girls tracks as loud as you want without any shame, this Korean-style
karaoke joint is the place. Open until 3am on weekends (perfect for when
inspiration strikes after last call), there are very reasonably priced private
rooms you and your friends can rent, and the song selection is current.
Trust me, they will have the most up-to-date feel good jams — they just
might not be in English. But not to worry; they'll have enough classics that
your entire group will be entertained all night long. Psst: there are multiple
microphones available. Belt it.

summerhill and rosedale

Formerly the estate of William Botsford Jarvis,
Rosedale is one of Toronto's oldest and wealthiest
suburbs. Case in point: the enclave was actually named
for the wild roses that grew on the Jarvis property in
the 1800s. These days, the streets are narrow and lined
with trees, and turn-of-the-century mansions sit in all
their magnificence on every corner. When taking a stroll
through here, it's hard not to get lost in the beauty of
it – houses are surrounded by picturesque ravines and
parks that make you feel as if you are far from the city,
when in reality you're only a few minutes from downtown,
a fact that makes this residential area that much more
covetable. Not far down Yonge Street is Summerhill,
a community centered around the North Toronto Railway
Station. Located close to upscale shops and an abundance
of green spaces, the neighborhood is one of the most
sought out. While the wild roses aren't as abundant as
they once were in the 1800s, the elegance still blooms.

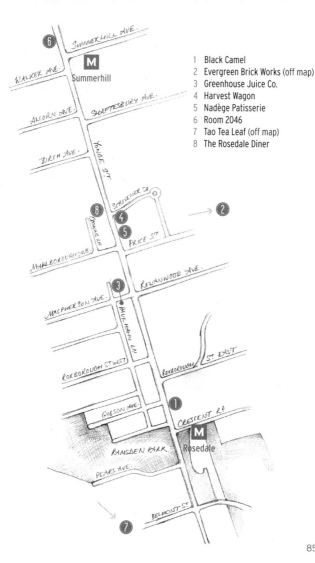

1 Black Camel
2 Evergreen Brick Works (off map)
3 Greenhouse Juice Co.
4 Harvest Wagon
5 Nadège Patisserie
6 Room 2046
7 Tao Tea Leaf (off map)
8 The Rosedale Diner

BLACK CAMEL

Consistently stellar sandwich shop

**4 Crescent Road (at Yonge Street) / +1 416 929 7518 / blackcamel.ca
Open daily**

You know you've arrived in this world when you don't need your name on the door. You might expect such honors to be reserved for members-only dining clubs or secret hotspots, but Black Camel is a nook of an eatery marked simply by an imprint of the desert-crawling friend. With lunch like this, who needs to flaunt it? Their secret to success is to know your customers and get it right every time. Black Camel's legendarily tender brisket marinates for three days before being roasted for 12 hours. Top it with caramelized onions and a touch of house-made barbecue sauce, and you'll have a recipe for instant cravings long after those seemingly never-ending lunch crowds fade.

EVERGREEN BRICK WORKS

Community environmental center

550 Bayview Avenue (near Pottery Road) / +1 416 596 7670
ebw.evergreen.ca / Open daily

Sometimes there's nothing better than finding an escape from your hometown in your hometown. The Evergreen Brick Works is a little oasis in Don Valley caught between expressways and electric towers. A one-time brick factory, the land is now used for workshops, ecological education programs, food truck festivals, kids' cooking classes and a farmers market that's become my Saturday wake-up call. It's also home to Café Belong, a restaurant that embodies the connection between food and land. Under the care of chef Brad Long, a salad is a thoughtfully balanced, local and sustainable delight. While it may not seem like the easiest place to get to if you're looking up directions on your phone, there's a shuttle bus that departs every 30 minutes from Broadview subway station.

GREENHOUSE JUICE CO.

Delicious and nutritious

5 Macpherson Avenue (near Yonge Street) / +1 416 546 1719
greenhousejuice.com / Open daily

Though I'm not a health nut, I want to go on record saying I've never had a more satisfying concoction in my life than the one I had here. Greenhouse Juice Co.'s organic, cold-pressed blends are found in cute glass bottles with kicky names, like Gold Rush and Rabbit, Run. If you're after something green, they have five options; I gravitate toward the Genius (cucumber, pineapple, celery, spinach, kale, lemon, E3 Live and Himalayan salt). Just want something tasty? Go for Wake Up (grapefruit, orange, lemon and liquid cayenne). If you don't want fruits and veggies, there's also nut milks (the Piloto with cold-brewed coffee, Brazil nuts, dates, vanilla bean and Himalayan salt is exemplary), immune boosters like The Flu Shot – a mix of echinacea, reishi, codonopsis, astragalus, oil of oregano and lemon – and hydrators such as the chia seed version made with alkaline water, maple syrup and lemon. Something for everyone.

HARVEST WAGON

Local grocer extraordinaire

1103 Yonge Street (near Scrivener Square) / +1 416 923 7542
harvestwagon.com / Open daily

Every time I'm in Summerhill, I make it a point to stop by this grocery store, even if it's to get a quick peek at the window display, which is always filled with gorgeously arranged fresh items. While this specialty market is small, the produce section is extra wonderful — the owners wake up before the sun every morning to handpick the goods from the Ontario Food Terminal and stock exotic varietals when in season. I've scored some truly incredible organic mangoes here. Each aisle provides ample inspiration for cooking: there's a huge selection of imported oils and vinegars to complement any of their fresh meats or fish. Don't have time to cook? Then grab a container of antipasto (you can't go wrong with marinated artichokes), eggplant parmigiana and a prepared chicken dish from their prepared foods counter.

NADÈGE PATISSERIE

Parisian-inspired, artistic desserts

1099 Yonge Street (near Price Street) / +1 416 968 2011
nadege-patisserie.com / Closed Monday

I have been charmed by Nadège Nourian's offerings for as long as I can remember. Her passion for good food, quality products and attention to the teensiest of details is something that I admire. One of the many reasons I love visiting her boutique bakery is the architecture: it's housed within a heritage building, and the shop shows off all of the original characteristics, including exposed brick walls. With no dine-in option available, the real focus here is well-made chocolates and baked goods. I suggest trying the Earl Grey and dark chocolate truffle, as well as the green tea and salted caramel macarons. You'll be craving more immediately.

ROOM 2046

Exclusive handmade gifts

1252 Yonge Street (near Summerhill Avenue) / +1 647 348 2046
room2046.com / Open daily

Room 2046 is equal parts boutique, design studio and espresso bar — a place that appeals to all the senses. This concept shop is truly a godsend when you're in need of a last-minute present in the area. I frequent it to check out the internationally sourced, intentionally curated goods, and tend to gravitate toward the housewares, books and jewelry. Among the items I've coveted are ceramics from HomArt Luna and clutches by Kias Leather, and on my last visit here, I purchased a candle holder in the shape of a sinking ship created by local designer imm Living. So perhaps the presents are sometimes for myself. Once you're here, you'll understand completely.

TAO TEA LEAF

An eclectic variety of camellia sinensis

934 Yonge Street (near Frichot Avenue) / +1 647 728 3858
taotealeaf.com / Open daily, Sunday by appointment

Who knew that there was so much to know about tea? I never did until my partner and his brother taught me there was more to cha than Earl Grey. They brought me to this showroom, co-owned by Tao Wu, a certifed tea sommelier and importer of some of the finest leaves from China, Japan, India, South America and Africa. Each visit, you'll be greeted and assisted with care and walked through the different brews – or ceramics, if you need hardware – that have come in. I highly suggest signing up for their Intro to Tea workshop; it's a fascinating look at history through the lens of what's in your cuppa.

THE ROSEDALE DINER

A hidden gem

1164 Yonge Street (at Scrivener Square)   +1 416 923 3122
rosedalediner.com   Open daily

The Rosedale Diner is an institution in Toronto. It's a cheerful establishment plating up food that will make you stand up and cheer. The décor hasn't changed since the 1960s, and there's an adorable outdoor patio filled with cherry-red chairs, dappled light and greenery. There are many expected diner options (hello, greasy hamburger!), as well as some surprising plates, like the upmarket duck poutine. I love coming here for breakfast in the summer and ordering the Bigger: three eggs, "all the meats" (meaning bacon, peameal bacon and sausage links), Israeli salad and Challa toast. So great.

downtown core

church and wellesley

Toronto's downtown is a world of fascinating contrasts. With a large concentration of skyscrapers and business towers, the skyline glows beautifully at night. Home to the CN Tower – once the tallest free-standing structure in the world – and Union Station, Downtown Core is one of the most vibrant and bustling places in the city. Nearby, there's Church and Wellesley, home to Canada's largest gay community and often called Gay Village. The enclave was established during the late 1960s when several queer-centered businesses and clubs opened, and has since thrived: it was a primary player in the much-loved HBO series *Queer as Folk* and is the host of this city's Pride Week, which typically draws a crowd of over a million supporters from around the world.

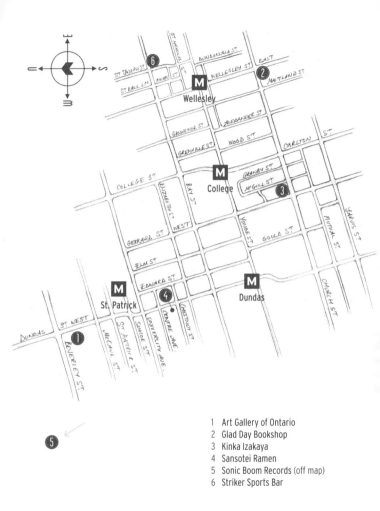

1 Art Gallery of Ontario
2 Glad Day Bookshop
3 Kinka Izakaya
4 Sansotei Ramen
5 Sonic Boom Records (off map)
6 Striker Sports Bar

ART GALLERY OF ONTARIO

A Gehry masterpiece

317 Dundas Street West (near Beverley Street) / +1 416 979 6648
ago.net / Closed Monday

When Frank Gehry returns to his hometown to construct an addition to a beloved city building, you stop and take notice. Nobody can say he didn't do a stellar job (you could sit in the stunning Galleria Italia all day), but it's another Canadian name that makes the gallery extra interactive. Once you've climbed through the Henry Moore sculpture out front (a rite of passage, really) and have seen the many treasures inside the main space including works by Andy Warhol, Evan Penny and Group of Seven, check out the Weston Family Learning Centre downstairs. It's basically a giant craft room with all the art supplies you could dream of – sure, it's for kids, but there's no reason you can't let your creativity flow, too. After all, you've just been inspired by Frank Gehry: any shape or design is possible.

GLAD DAY BOOKSHOP

Historic queer bookstore

499 Church Street (near Wellesley Street East) / +1 416 961 4161
gladdaybookshop.com / Open daily

There's a lot of history in Toronto's queer community, and one of the spots actively preserving it is Glad Day Bookshop. This store, specializing in LGBTQIA books, magazines and literature, has been a touchstone for many (myself included) since it opened in the 1970s. But this place is much more than a purveyor of the written word. I recently bought a shirt here declaring "More Fats, More Femmes," which I wear proudly everywhere I go. Additionally, this community hub hosts tawdry events, including erotic storytelling and NSFW coloring book gatherings.

KINKA IZAKAYA

Small plates, rowdy staff and lots of sake

398 Church Street (near McGill Street) / +1 416 977 0999
kinkaizakaya.com / Open daily

If you're a fan of Anthony Bourdain's *Parts Unknown*, then you may have caught the episode where he goes to Tokyo and explores izakayas. Heading to Kinka is exactly like that – without the 13-hour flight. Things can get a bit loud here, but grab an ice-cold Sapporo, watch the cooks in action and explore the shareable menu. Try the kurage (marinated jellyfish) to experience one of their most lip-smacking dishes, but if you're yearning for a classic, grab an order of chicken karaage, which is fried to crisp perfection and extra juicy!

SANSOTEI RAMEN

Slurp it up

179 Dundas Street West (near Chestnut Street) / +1 647 748 3833
sansotei.com / Closed Sunday

When the deep freeze of winter hits this city, it's a good bet that I will be
eating nothing but ramen for months on end. But not any ramen will do:
it needs to be the warm, rich broth from Sansotei. Many locals share this
sentiment, which means you're likely to be sharing a table with others in this
snug space. My go-to order is the tonkatsu black (garlic) ramen. It's creamy
and toothsome with the pork wonderfully cooked and noodle ratio just right.
The portion sizes are also just right, so you won't feel too stuffed. Up for a
taste test? Compare the juicy, tender, irresistible karaage to Kinka Izakaya's
(pg 98). Scrumptious fun for all.

SONIC BOOM RECORDS

A vinyl lover's dream

215 Spadina Avenue (near Sullivan Street) / +1 416 532 0334
sonicboommusic.com / Open daily

If you love LPs as much as I do (let's be honest, they do sound better), then you'll love Sonic Boom Records. It's easy to lose hours of your day exploring the store's collection of new and used albums, especially when you're nearly guaranteed to find some amazing gems (hey there, White Stripes *Hello Operator* 7" picture disc in excellent condition!) alongside some kick-ass local finds and everything a collector needs, including turntables, sleeves and more. But if records aren't your thing, this joint has so many knick-knacks and books related to music and pop culture that you won't feel left out.

STRIKER SPORTS BAR

A sports bar for the gay crowd

31 Saint Joesph Street (near Bay Street) / +1 416 929 9595
strikertoronto.com / Open daily

If there was one thing that was missing in the Gay Village, it was a place to watch sports. At least, that was the biggest thing that owners Oliver, Vince and Kevin noticed. Rather than complain, they did something about it and opened Striker Sports Bar, and I for one am glad they did. It's an open and inclusive space for all folks, and with a neon-lit bar, exposed duct work and black subway tiles, I daresay it's better looking than most other sports-centric watering holes around town. With tons of yummy food available (I suggest the nachos topped with melty queso fresco, mild aged cheddar, buffalo mozzarella, black beans, jalapenos, Kalamata olives and pico de gallo) and multiple HD screens showing myriad games at a time, Striker is a win no matter your team.

TORONTO AFTER DARK:
you can sip with us

Pick your poison

ARCHIVE
909 Dundas Street West (near St Mathias Place;
Little Italy), +1 647 748 0909, archive909.com
open daily

BAR RAVAL
505 College Street (at Palmerston Avenue; Little Italy)
+1 647 344 8001, thisisbarraval.com, open daily

BURDOCK
1184 Bloor Street West (at Pauline Avenue; Bloordale)
+1 416 546 4033, burdockto.com, open daily

CIVIL LIBERTIES
878 Bloor Street West (near Ossington Avenue;
Bloordale), +1 416 546 5634, civillibertiesbar.com
open daily

GET WELL
1181 Dundas Street West (near Lakeview Aveue;
Little Portugal), +1 647 351 2337, getwellbar.com
open daily

THE SHAMEFUL TIKI ROOM
1378 Queen West (at Cowan Avenue; Parkdale)
no phone, shamefultikiroom.com, open daily

ARCHIVE

No matter your tipple of choice, Toronto boasts a bevy of drinking establishments that cater to our thirst for superb drinks and distinctive experiences. If you're looking to have a quiet drink with a friend or a rambunctious booze-fueled evening out, our thriving bar scene proffers a number of places to sip and slosh.

For me, winter is wine season. It's a time for hibernating and drinking a deep-bodied red. When cold days roll around, my go-to is always **Archive**, an approachable, hip enoteca. Much of the wine list is devoted to Ontario-based vintners, and the glasses come in three-ounce and five-ounce pours – don't worry, you can order by the bottle as well. I love the Pearl Morissette's Cuvée Mon Unique gamay, which fills the mouth with rich and earthy dark fruits. That said, if you're here during the summer, try the citrusy Cave Spring's Dolomite Riesling – it's wonderful.

Though most people come to **Bar Raval** for the pintxos, I come for the cocktails and gorgeous surrounds – it feels a bit like being inside a Gaudì work. The drinks menu, developed by Michael Webster and Robin Goodfellow, includes libations with playful names like Velour Track Suit (gin, grapefruit, lime, green Chartreuse and egg white) and Jacques Fresco (Tío Pepe fino, Guerra Blanco wine, lime, frankincense, Cava and mint). But if you're feeling adventurous, have the bartender mix you a concoction of their choice – you won't be disappointed.

There's something lovely about **Burdock**. All white-washed brick with black accents and Einsten bulbs that glow warmly, this microbrewery-meets-music venue is owned and operated by a group of musicians and music lovers, so it's no surprise that it's community-run and artist-driven. There are usually six beers on offer, including their house-made Vermont Blonde, West Coast Pilsner and Meube Noir, as well as live music nightly.

Want to head to where the insiders go? Get thee to **Civil Liberties**, which attracts bartenders and mixologists. With a cheeky twist on speakeasies, the entrance is marked by a giant, glowing pineapple, and the drinks are exclusively bespoke. If you think it, they have it: rose petals, hops, eucalyptus, bitters – the possibilities are endless. That said, there's nothing wrong with simplicity; my cocktail du jour isn't too fancy, just crushed ice, whisky, cinnamon and orange bitters, and they do it exceptoinally well.

CIVIL LIBERTIES

Is a dive bar with cheap hooch and arcade games more your speed? Then there's no better place than **Get Well**. You'll immediately walk into the taproom and feel a hipster vibe with dim lights and loud music, but stick it out. They've got plenty of things to imbibe, including an amazingly curated craft beer selection of rotating drafts and bottles, which often includes brews from local joints Left Field Brewery (see pg 60) or Junction Craft Brewing as well as gluten-free options.

It's hard to ignore Toronto's current love for all things tiki, and **The Shameful Tiki Room** is only adding to the fervor. It's over the top, with carved totems, painstakingly sourced vintage posters and rattan covering every inch of the space. The tropical drinks, which will bowl you over – figuratively and literally. When I came with a group of friends, we ordered the Mystery Bowl, a rum-based concoction served in a huge light-up bowl. The best part though? A gong announces its arrival! Individual creations are just as tasty: try the Blue Hawaii, a slush with rum, vodka, pineapple, lemon, Curaçao and coconut milk, or the strong Tiki Puka Puka with rum, allspice and orange.

TORONTO AFTER DARK:
live out loud

Mic check, 1-2, 1-2

Looking for energy-packed performances by phenomenal entertainers? Toronto has you covered. No matter your mood or feeling, this city is bursting with talent, from live music to drag acts to comedy and burlesque. So get out there and support our local performers.

For as long as I can remember, **Comedy Bar** has been the prime place for rising comics to get their start. While you may be thinking that new comedians can be pretty awful, I assure you that the material coming from these improv and sketch shows are hilarious. With programming ranging from feminist comediennes to rap battles to stand-up, you'll have a variety of shows to choose from at affordable pricing.

Want the Vegas experience without going there? Head to dinner theater **Candyland**. You'll see everything from aerialists to contortionists to fire breathers. Still not convinced? The food is worthwhile and, hey, you'll have an experience you won't be able to stop talking about.

First and foremost, let's make this abundantly clear: **Bovine Sex Club** is not a sex club. With no signage and a bunch of garbage adorned to the front, this club is the granddaddy of Toronto's alternative and punk scene. Some incredible bands have made their debuts here, including Alexisonfire and Billy Talent, plus there's burlesque in between acts. It's quite the place. Did I mention the tiki bar on the roof? You'll never be bored here.

COMEDY BAR

Lee's Palace is a venue I've been visiting since high school, so it's hard to make people understand the intensity of my excitement when I recognized it in the movie *Scott Pilgrim vs The World*. It's those little things, right? This concert hall is rich in history and a staple in this town's music scene. The multifloor venue brings back many memories of my youth, and it's always fun to come back and enjoy the main stage for an indie show.

Everyone loves a good multipurpose space and it's why I love **Buddies in Bad Times Theatre**. Located in the heart of the Gay Village, this joint typically operates as a stage showcasing queer content, but on the weekends, they throw a mean dance party. Well-known drag queens have been known to host charity events, so do check the calendar to see what's happening.

Phoenix Concert Theatre is tiny, the inside is dark and the acts it brings in are amazing. Because of its small capacity numbers, it also gives you the ability to get up close and personal with some killer musicians. Seeing Tegan and Sara play here was truly unforgettable!

BOVINE SEX CLUB
542 Queen Street West (near Ryerson Avenue;
Queen West), +1 416 504 4239, bovinesexclub.com
open daily

BUDDIES IN BAD TIMES THEATRE
12 Alexander Street (at Maitland Terrace;
Church Wellesley), +1 416 975 8555
buddiesinbadtimes.com, closed Monday

CANDYLAND
619 King Street West (near Portland Street;
King West), +1 647 347 6400, thecandyland.ca
open Thursday through Saturday

COMEDY BAR
945 Bloor Street West (near Delaware Avenue;
Wallace Emerson), +1 416 551 6540, comedybar.ca
open daily

LEE'S PALACE
529 Bloor Street West (near Bagpipe Lane; The Annex)
+1 416 532 1598, leespalace.com, open daily

PHOENIX CONCERT THEATRE
410 Sherbourne Street (near Carlton
Street; Cabbagetown), +1 416 323 1251
thephoenixconcerttheatre.com, open daily

cabbagetown

corktown

———◆———

Once a slum, Cabbagetown is quickly becoming one of
Toronto's most budding neighborhoods. Dating back to the
1840s, the area derives its name from the Irish immigrants
who grew cabbage in their front yards. Walking through the
enclave, which is surrounded by Parliament, Wellesley and
Dundas Streets, you'll find many Victorian-style homes, and
believe me when I tell you the architecture is so beautiful,
it's impossible to resist the urge to snap tons of photos.
To the east is Corktown, one of Toronto's oldest districts and
another that was historically inhabited by Irish immigrants.
In recent years, Corktown has been experiencing a surge
of revitalization with an influx of new businesses sprouting
up and young families moving in. For all the changes it's
seen, nineteenth-century buildings like the Enoch Turner
Schoolhouse and St Paul's Basilica still exist, keeping some of
this community's Old-World charm intact.

1 Barsa Taberna
2 Kanpai Snack Bar
3 Maisonette
4 Roselle Desserts
5 The Chefs' House
6 The Market Kitchen

BARSA TABERNA

A taste of Spain

26 Market Street (near Front Street East) / +1 647 341 3642
barsataberna.com / Open daily

I have to gush about the décor in Barsa Taberna for a minute. Inhabiting a historical building, the restaurant retained the original stone archways, which make for a striking juxtaposition against the stunning mosaic made out of blue, yellow and clear wine bottles and contemporary furnishings. Dining here for the interior and ambiance would be reason enough, but, as it happens, the food is excellent, too. The menu provides a true variety of options executed in traditional Spanish style as well as a few that blend global flavors together seamlessly. The grilled octopus drizzled in aioli and served with charred potatoes and chorizo is a delight. Be sure to order a glass of blanco, rojo or Cava sangria.

KANPAI SNACK BAR

Taiwanese street food

252 Carlton Street (at Parliament Street) / +1 416 968 6888
kanpaisnackbar.com / Open daily

Kanpai owner Trevor Lui and I go way back. We both actually started out as event planners and originally met at a conference in St. Louis, where I complimented his incredible pink bowtie. Years later, we ran into each other while he was launching his own noshery, and it's been nothing but love and support between us ever since. Serving up Taiwanese eats, the spot is hiphop-themed, and the creations all have entertaining names – for instance, *Deep Fried Goldmember* (fried squid), *Piggie Smalls* (pork belly) and, my choice, *Sticky Fingaz* (sticky rice with pork, mushrooms, dried scallops and shrimp). You can't leave here without getting an order of their award-winning deep-fried chicken, slathered in kicky spices. It's definitely got some pop!

MAISONETTE

Petite boutique with tasty treats

12 Tank House Lane (near Trinity Street) / +1 416 618 6041
maisonettedistillery.ca / Open daily

Blink and you'll miss this teeny purveyor of splendid foodstuffs. Nestled in
The Distillery District and opened by resident chocolatier, Laura Slack, once
you find the shop you'll step into a well-curated wonderland of a retail store.
It's packed with wonderful artisanal goods, including her divine truffles and
artfully wrapped chocolate bars. The first time I wandered in here was during
The Distillery's Christmas Market and I found myself obsessing over the
Sloane Tea, Nude Bee Honey and handcrafted chocolates. Although the space
is small, it's jam-packed with luscious treats that you'll want to bring home.

ROSELLE DESSERTS

French delicacies

362 King Street East (at Trinity Street) / +1 416 368 8188
roselleto.com / Closed Monday and Tuesday

I met Roselle Desserts co-owner, Steph, when I was teaching social media to a small group of food industry business owners. She showed me some of the photos on her Instagram and I was so impressed with her branding work that I wasn't entirely sure she needed my help. The petite bakery is a labor of love for Stephanie and her partner Bruce. They have everything from cookies and caramels to crêpes, but the thing that I love most is a slice of their inventive, Milk Bar-inspired gateau, which includes their version of the famous New York bakery's birthday cake truffles. Have your cake and eat your truffles, too!

THE CHEFS' HOUSE

Student-made, upmarket fare

215 King Street East (at Frederick Street) / +1 416 415 2260
thechefshouse.com / Closed Saturday and Sunday

You won't discover a better culinary bang for your buck than The Chefs' House. Entirely run and operated by George Brown College, the restaurant is managed by budding hospitality management students and newly minted chefs. From appetizers to dessert you'll be extremely well taken care of, even if the staff does seem a bit nervous at times. The menu changes weekly, and there's always a pre-fixe with a choice of three or four courses, all entirely composed of local ingredients. I've had everything from sous-vide pork loin to pan-seared sea bream to house-cured trout gravlax. The food is very high-end, impeccably made and much friendlier on your wallet than other fine dining establishments in town.

THE MARKET KITCHEN

Mix and make

St Lawrence Market, 92-95 Front Street East (near Market Street)
+1 416 860 0727 / stlawrencemarket.com / Open Friday and Saturday

When it comes to whipping up a quick meal, the vendors at St Lawrence Market have kicked my imagination into high gear. But you know what's better than all those fresh, sustainable products? The Market Kitchen. Housed on the upper mezzanine in the South Building (the site of Toronto's first city hall), this is a venue for fantastic culinary classes and showstopping events. Sign up for a lesson here and you'll soon learn how to create serious plates with the help of trained chefs; though the instructors aren't named on the online schedule, they are sometimes noteworthy – I once was taught by Food Network Canada host and chef, David Adjey. Fun fact: all ingredients are sourced from the market's vendors.

leslieville and riverdale

In Toronto's ongoing east vs. west battle, the west usually comes out on top. But the east side — specifically Leslieville — has started to give the west side some real competition. It's even been deemed the Williamsburg of Toronto! Located to the east of Don River, the neighborhood used to be the home of many greenhouses and brick factories in the 1800s, but nowadays trendy urbanites looking to settle down are moving in, sharing their backyards, coffee shops and restaurants with the nearly ever-present film and television production crews who are constantly scouting for locations. Across the water is Riverdale, another multicultural, up-and-coming, east-end area. Historically, this community consisted primarily of Victorian- and Edwardian-style boarding rooms for the working class, and, fittingly, Toronto's first baseball stadium was built here. Swing by Leslieville and Riverdale, and give these burgeoning hoods a gander to see it all for yourself.

WOODFIELD RD
HIGHFIELD RD
GLENSIDE AVE.
REDWOOD AVE.
GREENWOOD AVE.
HERTLE AVE.
BILLINGS AVE.
DRUMMOND AVE.
ATHLETIC AVE.
GREENWOOD PARK
ALTON AVE.
HASTINGS AVE.
LESLIE ST.
GERRARD ST EAST
STRATHCONA ST EAST
DUNDAS ST.
JONES AVE.
CONDY AVE.
BERTMOUNT AVE.
CAROLINE AVE.
WINNIFRED AVE.
BROOKLYN AVE.
PAPE AVE.
HEWARD AVE.
BOSTON AVE.
CARLAW AVE.
COLGATE AVE.
VERRAL AVE.
BAIN AVE.
LOGAN AVE.
BOOTH AVE.
FIRST AVE.
McGEE ST.
BOULTON AVE.
QUEEN ST.

1 Arts Market
2 Belmonte Raw
3 Common Sort
4 Hooked
5 Lahore Tikka House
6 Queen Margherita Pizza
7 Saturday Dinette

ARTS MARKET

Handicrafts galore

1114 Queen Street East (at Caroline Avenue) / +1 416 546 8464
artsmarket.ca / Closed Monday and Tuesday

It's no secret that Toronto has a huge arts community, but did you know we have an equally robust craft community? Rather than wait for the holidays to find some well-made, one-of-a-kind pieces, owner Daniel Cohen wanted to create a space that gave makers the opportunity to sell their goods year-round. Thus, Arts Market was born. The venue itself is large and handsome, with a well-curated list of around 40 vendors ranging from paper goods created by Handmades by Rovena to fab-smelling bath products by Beauty in the Bath – no matter your heart's desire, you'll spy items for every style, be it kitsch or antique. Even better? It's all affordably priced. One of my grooviest finds here has to be a necklace made of found objects by Aminda Wood that jazzes up any outfit.

BELMONTE RAW

For all your cold-pressed juice needs

1022 Queen Street East (near Boston Avenue) / +1 647 340 1218
belmonteraw.com / Open daily

A few years back, I went to a culinary summer camp for adults. Yes, it was
as amazing as it sounds. Each morning, Belmonte Raw would deliver
our breakfast, providing granola and freshly pressed juices. Prior to this,
I was one of those people who thought all juice was weird and gross,
but guess what? I totally ate (or, drank, as it were) those words. The flavor
combinations from this shop are rich, but not overpowering, and range in
health benefits from detoxing to hydrating to strengthening your immune
system. For a pick-me-up, I love Jolt: it has cold-brewed coffee, almond milk,
bananas, cacao, maca, lucúma, maple syrup and vanilla bean. But if it's pure
fruit and veg you're after, try Refresh (carrot, apple, beet, lemon and ginger),
which is sweet and tangy.

COMMON SORT

For all your secondhand clothing needs

800 Queen Street East (near Boulton Avenue) / +1 416 463 7678
commonsort.com / Open daily

I am a sucker for all things vintage, and Common Sort is my very favorite consignment store in Toronto. For a plus-size, curvy girl like myself, it's hard to find duds from yesteryear that fit. But without fail, I have found – and purchased – many cute skirts, dresses and shoes here that fit oh-so right. Now keep in mind that you may have to do a bit of digging through the inventory, but the super reasonable prices are well worth the effort. What's more, the staff is always willing to help you find what you're looking for – they even make suggestions for putting an outfit together. One of my top scores was a stretch cotton floral dress with cap sleeves that is still in my closet. So perfect for the summer.

HOOKED

The knowledgeable fish store

888 Queen Street East (near Booth Avenue) / +1 416 825 9281
hookedinc.ca / Closed Monday

There's something to be said for focus. I'm that person constantly on the go, juggling five jobs and ten side projects. When I see someone with singular intent, I feel a wee bit envious. Hooked is all about seafood, and you'll be hard-pressed to find anyone in town better versed than husband-and-wife team Dan and Kristin Donovan and their expert staff. They go direct to the source, personally working with fishers, farmers and processors, and know where each oyster, salmon and perch is from and when it was caught. Short on ideas for how to prep that Arctic Char flown fresh from Washington State? Just ask. With trained chefs on hand, you'll not only leave with the catch of the day, but an arsenal of cooking tips. They got the name right, too.

LAHORE TIKKA HOUSE

Delish Pakistani fare

1365 Gerrard Street East (near Highfield Road) / +1 416 406 1668
lahoretikkahouse.com / Open daily

The aloo gobi (potato and cauliflower with turmeric) at Lahore Tikka House is reason enough to head to this hood. Plus, the experience of eating here shouldn't be missed. Picture patio furniture under a tent, foldaway interior tables and sizzling kebabs served on cast-iron cookware alongside Styrofoam plates and plastic forks. Though it's incredibly no-frills, this place stays so busy it doesn't need added word of mouth: the food is so scrumptious you'll be talking about it long after your visit. What's their trick? Talk of special spices seems veiled in secrecy, but the leafy cilantro and fresh green chilies add a welcome brightness and kick to each dish. That said, trying to suss it out is a lost cause – just go, and bring friends. Each serving is meant for two, but could easily feed a family.

QUEEN MARGHERITA PIZZA

Pies to battle over

402 Queen Street East, #8 (at Vancouver Avenue) / +1 416 466 6555
queenmargheritapizza.ca / Open daily

I am fully aware that the following declaration may place a price on my head, but that's how dedicated I am to proclaiming this truth: this pizzeria makes the premier Neapolitan-style pie in Toronto. The fancy designations here (Caputo TIPO "00" flour, San Marzano DOP tomato sauce) may impress a certain segment of foodies, but for me it comes down to a flawless melding of flavors and textures: chewy crust with a few blackened bubbles, sweet yet tart tomato sauce and ooey-gooey cheese. I tend to go for The Dominator (fennel sausage, rapini, smoked mozzarella and fried chili oil) and The Alla Campagnolo (mushrooms, Asiago, garlic, goat cheese, oregano and white sauce) – drastically different, but both have incredible depths of flavor. Come on now, let yourself salivate with me. For a west-ender to cross this far east, it's gotta be good.

SATURDAY DINETTE

A modern take on the diner

807 Gerrard Street East (at Logan Avenue) / +1 416 465 5959 saturdaydinette.com / Closed Monday

I met Suzanne Barr at a conference called Kitchen Bitches. She discussed how she worked at the YWCA to hire and train local women looking to enter the restaurant industry, and I made it my mission to trek out here and try Saturday Dinette. I was not disappointed. Though the menu sounds like it's chock-full of comfort foods, they're made with a healthy twist that won't turn your nose up. My all-time fave is the chicken and grits — berbere-spiced, citrus-herb-brined chicken served with plain grits and greens sautéed in garlic — but I always love the rainbow trout burger, which comes with potato rösti and an apple and radish salad. Pro tip: if you post on social media, Barr and her staff may send you a free dessert. It happened to me and my partner on our date night.

the great outdoors

The prettiest locales for greenery

Toronto is a city bursting with culture, art, food and nightlife. But what about experiencing nature? Here, it's easy to escape the hustle and bustle of city life without even leaving the Downtown Core. Get ready to explore and acquaint yourself with this town's lushest nooks and crannies.

You don't have to imagine a massive greenhouse filled with tropical foliage right in the middle of downtown; you can visit it. **Allan Gardens Conservatory** is a weirdly magnificent urban escape. Over a century and a half ago, George William Allan donated this five acre plot to the Toronto Horticultural Society. Though the original wooden structure was destroyed by fire in 1902, it was replaced with the current glass-dome pavilion – much dreamier. Filled with everything from hibiscus to banana trees, it feels otherworldly to have this garden right downtown. Free of charge, it's a good recipe for renewal.

If I could go back in time, the turn of the 19th-century seems wildly romantic – I think I'd really dig the innovation, boundless hope and grit. Since we don't have viable time travel (yet), stepping foot into **The Distillery District** is the next best thing. It's a throwback to the Industrial Age; a cobblestone village decked out with glorious redbrick Victorian architecture. Once home to the Gooderham and Worts distillery, this pedestrian-only center is now a hotbed of theaters, boutiques, galleries and restaurants, not to mention street festivals. Hop on over yourself for a step back in time.

Last summer I challenged myself to explore more of this great city. I'm so glad I did for many reasons, but topping that list is the discovery of the **Leslie Street Spit Trail**. Located in Tommy Thompson Park, the trail, which stretches out over five kilometers (around three miles), boasts cottonwood and poplar trees along its path, more than 300 species of birds and one of the most remarkable views of downtown.

If the urban crush becomes too much for you, visit **Riverdale Farms**. It's a hidden gem, with seven and a half acres of farmland hanging out right in the middle of the city. While it's mostly scenic with lots of buildings to explore and pretty trails to get lost on, one of the highlights is the cows, pigs and horses that live on-site year-round. Bonus: it's free. If you visit during the summer months, don't forget to check out their excellent farmers market.

A visit to **The Toronto Islands** is a fantastic day trip. After a short boat ride from Jack Layton Ferry Terminal, you'll arrive at one of three major islands – Centre, Ward's or Algonquin – with paths, bridges and boardwalks that connect them all. During the summer, I love visiting the topless beach at Hanlan's Point, biking the trails and enjoying a picnic, taking in the glorious views of the skyline across the water while enjoying the ambiance of the island.

ALLAN GARDENS CONSERVATORY
19 Horticultural Avenue (near Jarvis Street;
Church Wellesley), +1 416 392 7288
facebook.com/Allan-Gardens-Conservatory
open daily

LESLIE STREET SPIT TRAIL
Trailhead at 1 Leslie Street (near Unwin Avenue;
Leslieville), +1 613 396 3226, ontariotrails.on.ca
open daily

RIVERDALE FARM
201 Winchester Street (near Sumach Street;
Riverdale), +1 416 392 6794
facebook.com/RiverdaleFarmToronto, open daily

THE DISTILLERY DISTRICT
55 Mill Street (between Parliament and Cherry
Streets; Distillery District), +1 416 364 1177
thedistillerydistrict.com, open daily

THE TORONTO ISLANDS
Jack Layton Ferry Terminal, 9 Queens Quay
West (Yonge Street; Downtown Core), no phone
torontoisland.com, open daily